science Fair

j507.8
G17656

Science Fair Projects—
Planning, Presenting, Succeeding

Science Fair Projects—
Planning, Presenting, Succeeding

Robert Gardner

Enslow Publishers, Inc.

40 Industrial Road   PO Box 38
Box 398   Aldershot
Berkeley Heights, NJ 07922   Hants GU12 6BP
USA   UK

http://www.enslow.com

Library of Congress Cataloging-in-Publication Data

Gardner, Robert, 1929–
    Science fair projects—planning, presenting, succeeding / Robert Gardner.
       p. cm. — (Science projects)
    Includes bibliographical references and index.
    Summary: Provides information on choosing and planning a science fair project,
carrying it out, recording your findings, writing a report, and exhibiting the project.
    ISBN: 0-89490-949-5
    1. Science projects—Methodology—Juvenile literature. [1. Science Projects—
Methodology.] I. Title. II. Series: Gardner, Robert, 1929– Science projects.
Q182.3.G39   1999
507.8—dc21   98-8667
                                           CIP
                                           AC

Printed in the United States of America

10 9 8 7 6 5 4 3 2

To Our Readers:
All Internet addresses in this book were active and appropriate when we went to press. Any
comments or suggestions can be sent by e-mail to Comments@enslow.com or to the address
on the back cover.

Illustration Credits: Stephen F. Delisle

Photo Credits: AP/World Wide Photos, p. 21 (bottom); Martha Magane, p. 16.

Cover Photo: Jerry McCrea (foreground); © Corel Corporation (background).

MAY –– 2001
L/1

Contents

Introduction

An excellent way to get involved in science is to do a science fair project. This book is filled with suggestions about how to do your own science fair project. You will find out how to choose a topic, the types of projects you might do, how to plan your project, how to proceed in actually doing the work, and how to exhibit your project at a science fair. In the process of doing such a project, you will learn a lot about science and the scientific method.

Like any good scientist, you will find it useful to record your ideas, observations, data, and anything you can conclude from your experiments in a notebook. If your project involves numbers, it is likely that you will be making calculations. In that case, you will also find a pocket calculator very useful.

You should be aware that judges at science fairs do not reward projects or experiments that are simply copied from a book. For example, doing a classic experiment from a book that you have no fresh ideas about will not impress judges. However, an experiment that you designed yourself and that reveals relationships between variables you tested experimentally will probably be given close consideration. Your exhibit could include a detailed logbook with tables and graphs of data you collected.

If you decide to enter a science fair and have never done so before, you'll find this book helpful. You might like to consult some of the books listed in the Further Reading section as well. These books deal with science fairs or closely related topics. They will provide plenty of helpful hints and lots of useful information that will enable you to avoid the pitfalls that sometimes plague first-time entrants.

Safety First

Any science project that requires experimentation should be done with caution. Do not take chances or do anything that could be dangerous. If you feel the need to do an experiment that has any potential for danger, consult a knowledgeable adult and ask him or her to help you. Read and follow the safety rules listed below before you start any project.

1. Do any experiments or projects, whether from this book or of your own design, under the supervision of a science teacher or other knowledgeable adult.

2. Read all instructions carefully before proceeding with a project. If you have questions, check with your supervisor before going any further.

3. Maintain a serious attitude while conducting experiments. Fooling around can be dangerous to you and to others.

4. Wear approved safety goggles when you are working with a flame or doing anything that might cause injury to your eyes.

5. Do not eat or drink while experimenting.

6. Have a first-aid kit nearby while you are experimenting.

7. Do not put your fingers or any object other than properly designed electrical connectors into electrical outlets.

8. Never experiment with household electricity except under the supervision of a knowledgeable adult.

9. Do not touch a lit high-wattage bulb. Lightbulbs produce light, but they also produce heat.

10. Many substances are poisonous. Do not taste them unless instructed to do so by a knowledgeable adult.

11. Keep flammable materials such as alcohol away from flames and other sources of heat.

12. If a thermometer breaks, inform your adult supervisor. Do not touch either the mercury or the broken glass with your bare hands.

1

Getting Started

If you like science, you will enjoy doing a science project because you will gain a better understanding of what science is all about. You will also understand what it is like to work as a scientist.

Developing a project for a science fair, especially one that involves experiments, will help you sharpen skills that you will find useful whether or not you become a scientist or work in a science-related profession. You will learn to use your senses to make careful observations. Some of your observations will probably be quantitative; that is, you will take measurements using rulers, protractors, balances, micrometers, telescopes, microscopes, stopwatches, or other measuring devices. On the basis of your observations, you will make inferences—attempts to explain your observations—that you will then test experimentally. This procedure—observation, inference, testing, and drawing conclusions—is called the scientific method. Not all science fairs require a project that involves experiments. If you are just starting to learn about science, you might want to do a less demanding type of project. You will find a description of such projects in Chapter 2.

You will learn to classify various things such as plants, animals, minerals, and stars on the basis of their attributes: brightness, color, texture, size, hardness, etc. By observing, measuring, classifying, and experimenting, you may begin to see patterns emerging from what at first seemed like chaos. You may notice that the moon rises roughly an hour later with each passing day, and that a full moon appears on the eastern horizon at about the same time that the sun is setting on the western horizon. You may find that seeds require water, warmth, and air to germinate; that light travels in straight lines; or that the angles a mirror makes with rays of incident light and reflected light are equal. Such patterns will allow you to make predictions. You will know when to expect the moon to rise or be full, where seeds can be expected to germinate, and where to place a mirror so that you can see into an adjacent room.

To convey to others what you learn by doing a science project, you will use and improve your communication skills. Most science fairs require that a written report accompany each exhibit and that exhibitors be available to discuss their projects with visitors and judges.

All these skills—making observations and inferences, measuring, classifying, experimenting, seeing patterns, and communicating— are useful whether or not you become a scientist. These are skills that will help you cope with everyday events, work, and issues that you will encounter throughout your life.

Selecting a Topic or a Question

One of the most difficult parts of a science project is selecting a topic. But one thing is certain: You should choose a topic or a question that really interests you. Do not pick something just so you can say you did a science project. If you decide to enter a science fair, do it right and enjoy it. The only way to have fun doing what is going to be a lot of work is to investigate a topic or question about which you want to learn more.

Ronald D. Brown, Jr., won first place in his school's science fair by choosing a topic that interested him and conducting experiments that led to a solid conclusion.

The best project for you is one that you have thought about and puzzled over for some time. The fact that it occupies your mind indicates that it is of interest to you. So why not use the time you will spend on the project to try to answer a question that intrigues you? That question might be related to your hobby: Maybe you collect insects and would like to learn more about the life cycle of one of the butterflies in your collection. Perhaps you play baseball and would like to investigate the factors that make a ball curve or the best way to throw a ball from the outfield. If you like to work with your hands, you might build a model of a solar-heated house.

If you do not have a subject that has been on your mind for some time, you may find one by letting your imagination wander. A good time to do this is at night when you are trying to get to sleep. You may think of a topic as you drift off into dreamland. Perhaps you will awaken with an idea that came to you as you slept. If not, let your imagination go searching some more as you lie in bed before getting up. Some people generate better ideas in the morning than at night. Keep a notepad next to your bed so that if an idea does come to you, you can write it down. You may not remember it when you get up.

People often find a topic in an unexpected way. It might be during a walk in the woods, while watching a TV program, during a conversation with a friend or family member, or while daydreaming. If you are searching for an appropriate question to use as a project, it will be on your mind. You will be primed to receive any stimulus that might trigger an interesting idea.

If you can't think of a topic by using your imagination or if one does not come to you in an unexpected way, do not despair. There are other ways to find a project you would like to pursue. Sometimes a visit to a science museum or a zoo will help. You may find a question or see something there that sparks your interest. Another approach is to talk to a teacher, a parent, or a friend. Because they know you well, they may have suggestions that will help you. Talk to other people, too—your doctor, a nurse, a veterinarian, a scientist, an engineer, or an inventor.

Other places where you might find information leading to a project are colleges and universities, hospitals, nature centers, botanical gardens, government agencies, industries, and animal hospitals. There may be people at these places who will offer help. But you will probably have to call and make an appointment. Tell the general operator at the place who you are and what you want. The operator or the public relations office will probably know to whom you should speak. Be clear about what you want to ask. Bring a list of questions with you to your meeting so that you will be prepared and not waste the time of the person who has agreed to talk to you.

If you have access to a computer that is connected to the Internet, you might try surfing the Web. Perhaps you will find a suitable topic or an intriguing question there.

Your science textbook may help. Turn to a chapter that you found enjoyable. Skim it for ideas you might like to pursue. Examine some of the books suggested in the book's bibliography.

Librarians can also be very helpful. They will direct you to books with rich sources of ideas. By perusing some of these books, you may hit on a topic that will become a good science project. If the books are arranged according to the Dewey decimal system, you might like to browse the shelves where the science books are found. The numbers used to classify the books are found on their spines. The natural sciences (astronomy, biology, chemistry, mathematics, physics, etc.) will have numbers between 500 and 599; the useful arts (agriculture, engineering, gardening, etc.) will have numbers between 600 and 699.

Libraries also have magazines such as *Scientific American*, *Science News*, *Discover*, and some magazines for young people. These journals may contain articles that will spark an interest and lead to a question you can investigate. Skimming science encyclopedias may bring your eye to a topic that will stimulate your enthusiasm for a project. *The New Book of Knowledge* has articles on various fields of science. Browsing through these articles might lead to an idea. Most libraries have the *Encyclopedia Britannica*, but its articles are quite scholarly and often difficult to read. Both the *World Book Encyclopedia* and *Collier's Encyclopedia* are general references that are somewhat easier reading. *Encyclopedia Americana* provides good information about science and technology.

One useful source of ideas that your library may have is a collection of abstracts (short versions) of past projects from the International Science and Engineering Fair (ISEF). The abstracts, published by Science Service in Washington, D.C., will give you a sense of the projects that have been entered in national competition.

A town library, such as this one on Cape Cod, is a good place for local students to begin their research on science fair projects.

What Makes a Good Topic?

Your topic should focus on a single question that you can realistically investigate in the time available to you. Choose a topic for which you can obtain the equipment or resources you need. You might be interested in atomic isotopes, but it's not likely that you will have access to a mass spectrometer, which is used to separate and identify isotopes. However, your school may have all the equipment you need to measure the half-life of a particular isotope.

Do not select a topic that is too broad. "Protozoa" is much too general; however, "a way to measure the average size of paramecia" is a doable project.

Here is a list of topics. Can you identify the ones that could be done in the time available to prepare for a science fair? Which ones are too vague, difficult, or lengthy to be realistic projects?

16

- Plants.

- How does age affect the viability of different seeds?

- How does light affect the production of starch in geranium leaves?

- An experimental determination of the radii of protons and neutrons.

- Establishing the position of genes on the human chromosomes.

- How can the efficiency of a solar collector be determined?

- Animals of the desert.

- A comparison of the effectiveness of different commercial antacids.

- American forests.

- Which brand of paper towel is the best water absorber?

You probably realize that "plants," "animals of the desert," and "American forests" are much too general to be science fair projects. "An experimental determination of the radii of protons and neutrons" requires equipment that you probably would not be able to find, afford, or operate. On the other hand, "Which brand of paper towel is the best water absorber?" or "a comparison of the effectiveness of different commercial antacids" are projects that could be done at a reasonable cost and in a reasonable period of time.

The topics in this list are not original, but they give you a sense of the kind of project appropriate for a science fair. They require experimentation and a knowledge of the scientific method. Making a model, preparing a demonstration, doing a survey, writing a report based on reading, or repeating a classic experiment are acceptable projects in many science fairs. Such projects will not require scientific thinking but may be appropriate for someone just starting to learn about science. You will find more about the different types of science projects in Chapter 2.

Know the Rules

If you plan to exhibit your project at a science fair, check the rules for the fair before you settle on a topic. Most fairs have rules restricting entries. For example, experiments with vertebrate animals may not be allowed. Some fairs will require proof of supervision by a qualified adult; others do not allow projects that involve humans as subjects; and most require supervision by a scientist if the project involves genetic engineering. Practically all fairs will ask you to fill out an entry form.

What Judges Look For at a Science Fair

Although the rules vary from one fair to another, there are certain things that those judging the projects usually look for and rate. These include creativity, use of the scientific method, thoroughness, appearance of the exhibit, and the oral presentation if one is required. The judges try to make their assessments by reading the reports, viewing and studying the exhibits, and talking with the presenters. The two major factors in rating projects are creativity and use of the scientific method. Often, each of these constitutes at least one third of the points judges assign to a project. You may have a very attractive exhibit with lots of color, a well-constructed model, and beautiful photographs and drawings, but unless your project reflects creative and original ideas, you will not fare well from a competitive standpoint. Similarly, because judges look for procedures that are genuinely scientific, you will be more likely to impress the judges if you do a research project that requires careful experimentation.

On the other hand, you may not be interested in the competitive nature of the fair. Perhaps you enjoy the artistic, research, or historical aspects of projects. If so, a project that requires designing original experiments to answer a question or test a hypothesis may not be for you. If that is the case, make use of those skills you enjoy and have fun.

2

Types of Science Projects

Although some science fairs allow only projects that are original investigations, most local fairs accept a variety of projects. After all, not all scientists are or were experimental scientists. One of the most famous of all, Albert Einstein, used the experimental results of other scientists in developing his own theories of relativity and the photoelectric effect.

Types of Projects

The projects most often accepted at science fairs include displays or demonstrations, models, reports, surveys, and repeats of famous experiments, as well as original experimentation.

Displays and Demonstrations

Displays and demonstrations are some of the most common projects seen at science fairs. Such a project might be a collection of insects native to your region of the country, birds' nests made by different species, spiderwebs sprayed with light-colored paint and collected on cardboard, and so on. On the other hand, you might build a device that has a practical use, such as a pinhole camera. The photographs you take with it could be part of your exhibit. You might design and assemble a burglar alarm to install in your home, build a telescope, or grow organic vegetables.

At many science fairs you will see demonstration experiments. You might find a device that measures the expansion of metals or an apparatus that measures the acceleration of a falling object or of one pulled horizontally by a constant force. Another possible demonstration might show how photosynthesis can be detected in plants.

If you do a display or demonstration, try to be creative. Provide some related information that is interesting and not widely known. For example, if you prepare a display of fossils, you could separate those that are of local origin. You might also provide a map and photographs of the area where they were found, along with information on the geology of that region and how the age of the fossils can be estimated.

Models

Models can be made from cardboard, wood, wire, clay, plaster of Paris, or sheet metal. The most common ones are of the solar system, the human eye, and volcanoes. Models such as these, however, require relatively little creativity. On the other hand, a model solar collector that heats and circulates water or a computer model of an aerodynamically superior airplane wing might be prizewinning entries.

Models certainly play a vital role in architectural structures, including the design of space stations. Buckminster Fuller made models of his now famous geodesic (lightweight and supported by tension) domes before any house-size domes were built. Near the sculpture of Crazy Horse that is being carved from a mountainside in South Dakota, there is a model showing what the much larger structure will look like when completed.

Models played a major role in the work of Nobel Prize-winners James Watson and Francis Crick in their explanation of the structure of DNA (deoxyribonucleic acid). Using the results of experiments conducted by M. H. F. Wilkins and Rosalind Franklin, Watson and

In South Dakota visitors can see a model of the sculpture of Crazy Horse (top) that is being carved in a nearby mountain (bottom).

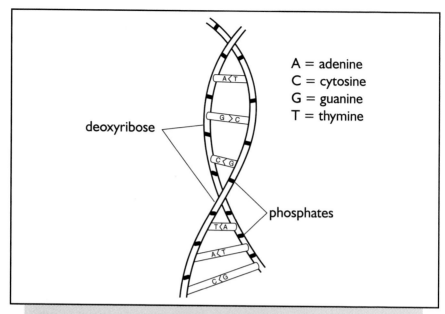

A = adenine
C = cytosine
G = guanine
T = thymine

deoxyribose

phosphates

Figure 1. Part of a model of a DNA molecule is shown. Notice how the spiraling strands of deoxyribose are linked by the amino acids adenine, cytosine, guanine, and thymine.

Crick developed a model of the DNA molecule (Figure 1) that revealed how it could transmit the genetic code.

Reports

Reports involve library and Internet research on the subject that interests you. The report, together with photographs, drawings, and other illustrations, becomes your display at the science fair. Some reports that have appeared at science fairs include *The Many Species of Whales, How Glass Is Made, The Similarities and Differences Between Eyes and Cameras, How Bees Communicate, The History of the Space Shuttle,* and *How Detectives Obtain Fingerprints.*

Surveys

You can conduct surveys of almost anything, from the favorite foods of the students in your school to the area's choice of candidates in a presidential election. A survey is not as easy to do as you might think. Questions must be carefully phrased to avoid ambiguity, enough data must be collected to make the findings meaningful, and statistical methods have to be applied to determine the significance of the results. Consequently, if you plan to do a survey, you will have to test your questions first to see how people interpret them. Then, you will have to spend many hours collecting data unless you can find people willing to help you. Finally, you will have to learn something about statistics (a math teacher can probably help you).

Performing a Famous or Classic Experiment

Some science fair projects are repeats of famous experiments performed by early scientists such as Archimedes, Galileo, Boyle, Charles, Newton, Faraday, Helmholtz, and others. The exhibitor's results can be compared with those of the original scientist. Sometimes the units used by the scientist are no longer in use, which poses an interesting problem. The old units must be converted into units we use today so that the two sets of data can be compared. Interest can also be added by giving the experiment a slightly different twist, showing how the experiment has led to practical applications in today's world, or describing how the experiment might be done with today's technology.

One famous experiment you might like to duplicate was performed by Eratosthenes (c. 276–c. 194 B.C.), who found a way to measure the earth's circumference. Eratosthenes lived in Alexandria, Egypt. He knew that in Syene, a city 500 miles south, there was a deep well in which a reflected image of the sun could be seen at noon on the longest day of the year. He realized that for this to happen, the sun must be directly over the well. It occurred to him that he could estimate the circumference of the earth by making some measurements on that longest day. He measured the length of the shadow of a tall tower in Alexandria at midday when the sun was directly overhead in Syene. The tower, which was 50 feet 9 inches tall, cast a shadow that was 6 feet 7 inches long (see Figure 2).

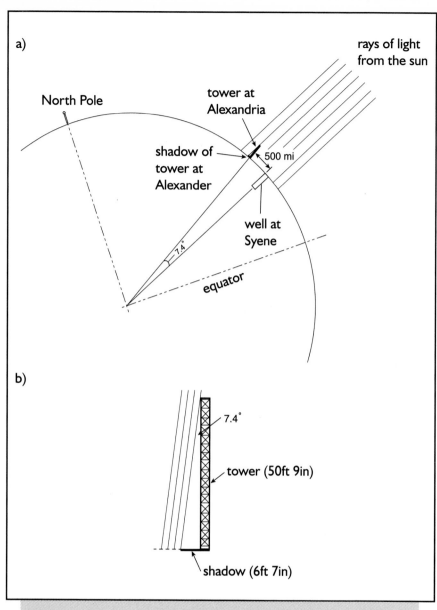

a)

rays of light
from the sun

North Pole

tower at
Alexandria

shadow of
tower at
Alexander

500 mi

well at
Syene

7.4°

equator

b)

7.4°

tower (50ft 9in)

shadow (6ft 7in)

Figure 2. a) A view through a section of the earth showing the sun over the well at Syene and the tower at Alexandria with its shadow. Both the well and the tower are greatly enlarged on this unscaled drawing. b) A more detailed drawing of the tower at Alexandria and its shadow. Unlike the sunlight at Syene, the sun's rays at Alexandria are not perpendicular to the earth's surface. They strike the ground and the tower at an angle of 7.4 degrees.

Using the data he had collected, Eratosthenes drew a simple triangle and measured the angle that the sun made with the tower. If you make a very careful drawing using Eratosthenes' data, you will see that the angle is a little more than 7 degrees. In fact, it is just about 7.4 degrees. Eratosthenes reasoned that if the sun's angle to the earth changed by 7.4 degrees in 500 miles, then it would change 360 degrees (one earth circumference) in 25,000 miles. The fraction of the earth's circumference, in degrees, between Alexandria and Syene must be 7.4° ÷ 360°, or 0.021. Therefore, he reasoned, the distance from Syene to Alexandria must be about 1/50 of the earth's circumference. Since 50 x 500 miles = 25,000 miles, he estimated the earth's circumference to be 25,000 miles. (Despite what you may have heard, people knew the earth was spherical long before Columbus.) However, Eratosthenes did not use miles or kilometers as his unit of measurement. Part of your project could be to find the units he used and convert them to present-day units.

You could also make your own determination of the earth's circumference. *The Old Farmer's Almanac* gives the sun's declination for every day of the year. The declination of the sun is its position north or south of the equator. At the spring and fall equinoxes (about March 21 and September 21), the sun is almost directly above the equator. At that point its declination is approximately 0 degrees. At the summer and winter solstices (about June 21 and December 21), the sun reaches its northernmost and southernmost positions. On or about June 21, the sun lies directly above a line of latitude 23 degrees 27 minutes (23°27') north of the equator. On or about December 21, it is over a line of latitude 23. 27° south of the equator.

How can you use the sun's declination and the shortest shadow cast by a vertical stick at your latitude to determine the earth's circumference? (It may help you to know that each degree of latitude is about 111 km, or 69 miles.)

Original Experimentation

Original scientific research usually involves trying to find the answers to questions through experimentation. Such an investigation is called original because you do not know the answer to your question. Your research may be original to you even if someone else has already answered the question. As far as you are concerned, the experiments that you design are original if you do not have an answer. Of course, you still may not know the answer when you finish your project. It is not unusual for a scientist to conclude that his or her experiment did not provide the information needed to answer the original question. However, the experiment may have provided some insight about how to proceed in developing another investigation that may lead to an answer. There is nothing wrong, therefore, in concluding that your experiment did not provide the answer you sought. It would be prudent in such a case to suggest another approach that might provide an answer.

Try to choose a research project that is limited in scope so that it can (1) be completed in a reasonable period of time, and (2) be approached experimentally. Be sure you can obtain and use any necessary equipment. For example, you could probably plan experiments that would enable you to answer the following questions:

- Which brand of paper towel is the strongest?

- Which brand of flashlight batteries lasts the longest?

- Does the size of raindrops change during a storm?

- What factors determine the lifting strength of an electromagnet?

On the other hand, you would probably not be able to carry out experiments that would answer the following questions:

- What happens to the molecular structure of water at temperatures close to absolute zero (–273°C)?

• What forms of life can be found in the deepest parts of the ocean?

Which Type of Project Should You Do?

If you have never done a science project before and have not studied science for very long, you should probably consider doing a report or a demonstration, building a model, or repeating a famous experiment. These projects generally require less time and can be more easily planned than original research or a survey.

If you enjoy mathematics, you might prefer doing a survey. Before you make that decision, be sure the rules of the fair allow you to do projects that involve humans. It would also be wise to talk to a math teacher or someone who can help you with any statistics that may be required to analyze the data you collect.

Research involving experimentation is much more time-consuming and difficult to plan because of all the obstacles you may encounter. However, you will learn more about science through experimentation than through other types of projects. Do you enjoy science? Are you deeply interested in a question that can probably be answered by experimentation? Do you have access to the equipment you will need? If your answers to these questions are yes, then you should seriously consider doing an experiment. Even if you do not complete the project, you can exhibit what you have done or continue the project and enter it in next year's fair or, perhaps, a national competition (see "Science Competitions and Organizations" on p. 97).

Some Possible Projects

Some possible topics for a science fair follow. Some are appropriate for original research involving experiments; others would make good subjects for surveys, demonstrations, models, or reports. A few are famous experiments that you could repeat. Although you probably won't do any of the ones named here, they may give you an idea for a related project.

Projects Related to Commercial Claims

- A survey: Do people prefer one brand of soda to another? Can they really tell the difference?

- Determine whether people can distinguish margarine from butter by taste.

- Find out if color affects the sales of a product. For example, does one automaker sell more blue cars than red cars?

- Determine whether one brand of hair curlers works better than others for all types of hair.

- Study whether you get more miles per gallon from one brand of gasoline than from others.

- Determine the conversion factors from metric to English, using labels on packages.

- Show whether it is less expensive to prepare pancakes using a packaged mix or to start from scratch.

Projects Related to Weather

- Measure the size of raindrops.

- Convert inches of snowfall into inches of rain.

- Photograph lightning.

- Perform French scientist Blaise Pascal's seventeenth-century experiment showing that air pressure decreases with altitude.

- Show how humidity affects the rate at which water evaporates.

- Show how snowflakes can be preserved.

- Explain why footprints made on frost-covered grass are often etched there for a prolonged period.

Projects Related to Heat and Temperature

- Determine how much heat is needed to melt a gram of ice.

- Show what happens to ice under pressure.

- Perform the classic experiments of eighteenth-century Scottish chemist Joseph Black that measure the heat needed to boil water or melt ice.

- Perform the classic experiment of eighteenth-century American-born scientist Count Rumford that showed that caloric (heat) had no mass. Early scientists thought heat (caloric) was a fluid.

- Demonstrate whether hot water freezes faster than cold water.

- Show how the expansion of different solids, liquids, and gases is related to temperature.

- Explain how the rate of heat transfer is related to surface area.

- Show how flame temperatures can be measured without a thermometer.

- Determine which materials make the best insulators.

- Explain what R values for insulation are and how they can be measured.

- Build a model solar home.

- Show how to make ice cubes that have no air bubbles.

- Build a solar heater that will heat a room.

- Distill water with sunlight.

Projects Related to Astronomy

- Discover a method for finding true north.

- Map the sun's path across the sky at different times of the year.

- Map the orbit of Venus.

- Measure the size of the sun and the moon.

- Determine the number of stars you can see in the sky on a clear night.

- Photograph the circumpolar constellations.

• Evaluate the evidence for the existence of UFOs.

• Explain the solar constant and how it can be measured.

• Determine the brightness of a full moon.

Projects Related to Light

• Explain why the shape and size of a reflected beam of sunlight change with the distance from the mirror.

• Study the images seen in plane and curved mirrors and why they are where they are.

• Explain how the path of a narrow beam of light can be bent.

• Determine whether the index of refraction of a substance is related to its density.

• Study whether a mirage can be created and explain how it happens.

• Duplicate Newton's classic experiments with a prism.

• Explain why some shadows are sharp and others are fuzzy.

• Explain why we sometimes see shadows that are colored.

• Determine whether light can be bent by magnets.

• Study how cylindrical lenses bend light.

• Measure the speed of light in different substances.

• Explain why fog lights are yellow.

• Explain what objects on land look like to a fish in water.

Projects Related to Chemistry

• Determine the percentage of oxygen in air.

• Determine how gases can be weighed.

• Determine how the components of mixtures can be separated.

• Devise a method to identify different metals.

- Measure the acidity of rain.

- Identify acids and bases, using natural indicators.

- Determine the thickness of a molecule of oleic acid.

- Determine the approximate volume of a molecule of water.

- Make large or long-lasting soap bubbles.

Projects Related to Physics

- Show how to measure friction.

- Demonstrate the frictional force between two surfaces.

- Perform Galileo's classic experiments with pendulums.

- Map the paths of projectiles and baseballs.

- Demonstrate nineteenth-century Danish physicist Hans Christian Oersted's discovery that a magnetic field surrounds an electric current.

- Verify nineteenth-century German physicist Georg Simon Ohm's discovery that for any given resistor the electric current through the resistor is proportional to the voltage across it.

- Repeat Michael Faraday's nineteenth-century discovery of electrical induction.

- Compare the "bounciness" of different balls.

- Demonstrate English scientist Robert Hooke's famous seventeenth-century experiment that led to Hooke's law.

- Test the efficiency of your bicycle.

- Measure and test different substances for electrical conductivity.

- Build batteries (electric cells) from natural materials.

- Show how electrical energy can be measured.

- Explain what a voltmeter measures.

- Demonstrate one way that electricity can be generated.

- Measure velocity and acceleration with a strobe light and camera.

- Measure the speed of sound.

- Measure the wavelength of sound or light.

- Test how temperature affects the shelf life of flashlight cells.

- Generate electricity with your bicycle.

- From big to small and back again: show the physics of scaling.

Projects Related to Biology

- Study the methods plants use to distribute seeds.

- Separate the pigments in leaves.

- Study how plants can be cloned.

- Duplicate Francesco Redi's classic experiment disproving spontaneous generation.

- Determine under what conditions plants grow best.

- Show evidence of photosynthesis experimentally.

- Explain how birds establish territories.

- Study the behaviors characteristic of mealworms, sow bugs, or earthworms.

- Study how the respiration rate of fish is affected by temperature.

- Identify animals by their tracks.

- Explain what we can learn from the patterns found in animal tracks.

- Determine the differences, if any, between white eggs and brown eggs.

- Try to follow the trail of a snail.

Katie Linarducci and Megan MacPhee completed a science project related to physics—they constructed a crystal radio.

- Explain how migrating animals navigate.

- Try to control the blooming of long- and short-day plants.

- Study the relationship between the heart rates of different animals and their size.

Projects Related to Humans

- Measure human power.

- Measure human reaction time.

- Muscles come in pairs. Compare their relative strengths.

- Study the relationship between body balance and vision.

- Study the relationship between peripheral vision and color vision.

- Study the speed of your reflexes.

- Study the factors, if any, that affect the growth rate of fingernails.

- Determine how much air you breathe.

- Determine the thickness of your hair.

- Determine how detectives lift fingerprints and describe what tools they need.

- Explain why two eyes are better than one.

3

The Scientific Method

Doing a science project, particularly one that involves original research, will require you to use the scientific method. In many textbooks you will find a section devoted to the subject. It will probably tell you that the scientific method consists of a series of steps. The book may even list the steps in a particular order, such as

- Realize that a problem or question exists.

- Form a hypothesis (an educated guess) about the solution or answer.

- Carry out an experiment or experiments to test the consequences of the hypothesis.

- Analyze the results of the experiment or experiments, looking for patterns.

- Draw a conclusion based on the data you have collected.

- When a number of hypotheses have been tested by experimentation in any one area, it may be possible to develop a theory or law that explains a great many related phenomena. For example, Newton's three laws of motion can explain all motion. The atomic theory of matter is the basis of modern chemistry.

While such a cut-and-dried explanation may appeal to someone starting out in science, any scientist will tell you that there is no set pattern that leads him or her to new knowledge. Each investigation is unique and requires different techniques, procedures, and thought processes. Perhaps the best description of the scientific method was given by Nobel Prize-winning physicist Percy Bridgman. He said that it was doing one's best with one's mind, no holds barred.

The idea that there is a set scientific method that all scientists follow probably came about because of the way scientists report their findings. These reports are similar in format and include the problem, the hypothesis, the experimental procedure, the results, and a conclusion. You will follow a similar format when you prepare the report on your project. First, you will refer to authority (search the literature) and come up with a question and a hypothesis. Next, you will conduct experiments in which you establish experimental variables and controls and make observations. Then, you will repeat experiments and determine any errors and their sources.

Referring to Authority

The first thing most scientists do before they develop hypotheses is to read what is already known about the subject they are investigating. If you are doing a report, you will probably not go beyond this step. You will collect information about the subject of your report by taking notes on what you read and then use that information to write a paper. If you quote someone else in your paper, be sure to provide a footnote. You will find information about footnotes in Chapter 6.

You read about sources of information when the question of choosing a topic was discussed in Chapter 1. Start with your library's computer catalog or card catalog and an index of magazine articles.

A librarian can show you how to use the library's resources. If you find that a great deal of information is available, you may feel overwhelmed because you know you can't read it all. Relax, you do not have to read everything. Here are some skim reading techniques that will make your task a lot easier.

- Look at the cover, title page, and the copyright page (the back of the title page). What was the date the book or magazine was published? If it is not reasonably recent, do not read it unless it details the history of your topic. It may contain information that has been updated by new work in the field.

- If it is a recent book, skim the introduction and the table of contents. Look for key words that tell you whether or not it has material that will be useful to you. Do the same with the index. If it is a magazine article, you can probably tell whether it will be useful by reading the first few paragraphs. If it is an Internet site, make sure the organization posting it is reputable. For example, sites from museums, colleges, or government agencies can usually be trusted for accuracy.

- Skim the appendix (if there is one) and the bibliography. The appendix may contain some valuable information. The bibliography may list some related books that you will want to read.

- When you find chapters or sections related to your topic, read those. Skip the rest.

- Take notes on your reading. Write your notes on index cards. At the top of the card write the name of the book, the author, the publisher, the place where it was published, and the date of publication. For an Internet site, note the URL, title and author of the article, the date it was posted, and the date you accessed it. You will need this information for your bibliography. As you write your notes, put the author's ideas into your own words. If you decide you might like to quote something the author has written, put the page number next to the quote so that you will have all the information you need when it is time to write a footnote in your final report.

A personal interview, face-to-face or by telephone or e-mail, can be an asset to your project. If you find a knowledgeable person who is willing to talk to you, prepare in advance. Think out and jot down significant questions. Arrange to use a tape recorder, and if your subject is willing, record your conversation. If the person is unwilling to be taped, you can jot down his or her ideas on index cards as the interview proceeds.

Developing a Hypothesis and a Question

After reading the literature, a scientist may develop a hypothesis. The hypothesis is his or her best guess at an answer to the question or problem. For example, about four hundred years ago Galileo hypothesized that an object's rate of fall is independent of its mass.

Your hypothesis might be: "The lifetime of a soap bubble is related to the concentration of glycerin in the solution used to make the bubbles." Perhaps you arrived at this hypothesis after reading articles for making long-lasting bubbles and found that one ingredient repeatedly listed was glycerin. Your hypothesis may be even simpler: "Different brands of paper towels absorb different amounts of water." Perhaps you arrived at this hypothesis by noticing that in your kitchen some brands of paper towels seem to be used up more quickly than others.

For many science fairs, you have to follow a format in writing your report. The format may require that you state the problem or question you are investigating. The problem is really your topic, the subject of your project. You can usually state the problem by rewriting the hypothesis. In the examples above, Galileo's problem would have been: "Does the mass of an object affect the rate at which it falls?" Your two problems would be: "Does the concentration of glycerin affect a soap bubble's lifetime?" and "Do different brands of paper towels absorb different amounts of water?"

In real life, you may think of the hypothesis before you consider it as a problem or question. Perhaps you thought that you would like to do something related to soap bubbles as a science project. Using different paper towels to clean up spills may have led you to hypothesize that some brands of paper towels absorb better than others.

Experimenting

Your project will involve experimenting if you are doing original research or repeating a famous experiment. Let's assume that your question is, "How is the period of a pendulum affected by the mass of the bob?" (The period is the time required for the bob to make one complete swing back and forth.) Your hypothesis is, "The period of a pendulum increases as the mass of the bob increases." This hypothesis seems reasonable to you because you expect a large mass, such as a bowling ball, to move more sluggishly than a small mass, such as a baseball.

To carry out the experiment, you find a number of different masses of the same size, such as the metal balls with hooks shown in Figure 3a. You attach one of the masses—an 18-gram aluminum bob—to a string that is suspended from a clamp, as shown in Figure 3b.

Variables

In order to test your hypothesis experimentally, you must recognize the variables in your experiment. The independent variable, the one that you will change and manipulate, is the mass of the bob. The dependent variable, the one that you expect to be affected when the independent variable changes, is the period of the pendulum. Again, the period is the time it takes for the bob to make one complete swing or oscillation back and forth (Figure 3c). All the other variables, the controlled variables, should remain unchanged. These include the length of the pendulum, which is the distance from the

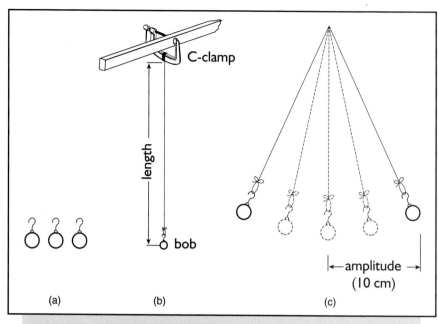

Figure 3. A pendulum project: a) Metal balls with hooks serve as bobs. The balls are all the same size but are made of different metals, so their masses are different. b) A bob is suspended from a string that is clamped to a supporting frame. The length of the pendulum is measured from its point of suspension to the center of the bob. c) A pendulum's period is the time it takes to make one complete swing (oscillation) over and back. Its amplitude is the distance from the center to either end of its swing.

point of support to the center of the bob, and the amplitude, which is the distance that the bob moves from its rest position as it swings. The size of the bob, your location on the earth, the temperature, and the humidity are other controlled variables. Of course, if you repeat the experiment in the same place over a relatively short time, all the variables other than the mass of the bob and the period should remain unchanged. That way they have no effect on the experiment.

You decide to keep the length of the pendulum fixed at 1.0 m and make the initial amplitude of swing 10 cm by pulling the bob back 10 cm before releasing it (Figure 3c). You begin by using a stopwatch to measure the bob's period; that is, the time to make one complete swing over and back, a total distance of 40 cm. You repeat this a number of times and record the results in a table like Table 1.

Table 1: The period of a 1.0-m-long pendulum with an 18-g aluminum bob and an amplitude of 10 cm.

Trial	Period (s)
1	2.09
2	2.02
3	2.10
4	2.00
5	2.12
6	1.95
7	2.16
8	1.96
9	2.15
10	1.94

Average period = 20.49 s ÷ 10 trials = 2.05 s ± 0.11 (The values vary from 2.16 s to 1.94 s, which are 0.11s greater and less than the average value of 2.05 s.)

Based on the data, you decide that measuring the time for one swing or oscillation is not very accurate. The results show that the average time you measured was 2.05 s ± 0.11. This means you can only measure the period to within about 5 percent [(0.11 ÷ 2.05) x 100].

You realize that it is difficult to start the watch at the precise moment you release the bob and stop it at the exact moment it returns to its starting point. You think your results will be more precise if you measure the time it takes the pendulum to make 20 swings. Over a time of about 40 seconds, the small timing error in

Table 2: The period of a 1.0-m-long pendulum with an 18-g aluminum bob and an amplitude of 10 cm. The period was obtained by dividing the total time by 20.

Trial	Time (s)	Number of oscillations (n)	Period (s/n)
1	40.10	20	2.01
2	40.05	20	2.00
3	40.08	20	2.00
4	40.12	20	2.01
5	40.14	20	2.01

starting and stopping the watch should become negligible. The results you obtain (Table 2) confirm your decision.

Now that you can measure the period with good precision, you change the mass of the bob (the independent variable) to see what effect it has on the period (the dependent variable). But first you make certain that the length of the pendulum is still 1.0 m when you hang a 47-gram zinc bob from the string. You find that you have to make a slight adjustment to keep the length of the pendulum at exactly 1.0 m. You make the adjustment, pull the bob 10 cm to the side, and release it as you start the stopwatch. You do the experiment 5 times and obtain the results shown in Table 3.

If you find that your results do not confirm your hypothesis, make a note of this beneath your data table. To see if a still larger mass will have an effect, you use a 76-gram lead bob and repeat the experiment once more. Your results, shown in Table 4, confirm your earlier experiment. The mass of the bob seems to have no effect on the period of a pendulum. You make a note of this again with a reminder that you will want to return to your results later and try to figure out why your hypothesis was incorrect.

Table 3: The period of a 1.0-m-long pendulum with a 47-g zinc bob and an amplitude of 10 cm. The period was obtained by dividing the total time by 20.

Trial	Time (s)	Number of oscillations (n)	Period (s/n)
1	40.12	20	2.01
2	40.04	20	2.00
3	40.10	20	2.01
4	40.09	20	2.00
5	40.14	20	2.01

Table 4: The period of a 1.0-m-long pendulum with a 76-g lead bob and an amplitude of 10 cm. The period was obtained by dividing the total time by 20.

Trial	Time (s)	Number of oscillations (n)	Period (s/n)
1	40.14	20	2.01
2	40.10	20	2.01
3	40.10	20	2.01
4	40.00	20	2.00
5	40.04	20	2.00

The experiments illustrated by this example of a pendulum project have included careful observations that have been both qualitative and quantitative. The experimenter watched the pendulum swing back and forth (qualitative) and measured the pendulum's period (quantitative). Those numbers were used to discover that the period is not affected by the mass of the bob. To be more certain of the conclusion, you could repeat the experiments several times to see whether the results are similar.

Scientists, particularly inventors, will sometimes resort to a trial-and-error approach to find an answer to a question or a solution to a problem. Thomas Edison tested 1,600 different filaments in an effort to design a lightbulb that would last long enough to make electricity a practical and economical way to light homes. If you wanted to answer the question, "How can I change the period of a pendulum?" there are a number of different factors you might change. You might try changing the pendulum's length, its amplitude, the size of the bob, the thickness of the string, and other variables to see which ones, if any, affect the period.

Science When Experiments Are Not Possible

Most people would agree that astronomers are scientists, yet astronomers cannot conduct experiments in a laboratory. They cannot manipulate or even touch the stars they study. They must depend on observations of things as they exist and watch patiently to see how naturally occurring variables affect stars, planets, moons, asteroids, and so on. Despite their inability to conduct direct experiments, astronomers do make careful measurements. For example, by observing and measuring the wavelengths of light emitted by stars, they can determine the elements that make up the stars and the speed at which the stars are moving away from us.

Conducting direct experiments is often impossible in medical research and other fields such as sociology, anthropology, and much of human psychology. Scientists working in these fields do the best they can by making careful observations and trying to be as objective as possible.

Surveys are not experiments in the usual sense, but scientists use surveys to collect information. In direct experiments a scientist changes the independent variable to see what effect it has on the dependent variable. In surveys the questioner generally tries to find out what people believe or feel or do. Questions are carefully phrased to avoid changing the thinking or behavior of the people being surveyed.

Surveys may provide answers to questions that cannot be obtained by experiment. For example, are the children of parents who both went to college more likely to graduate from college than the children of parents who did not attend college? It would be impossible to take a large group of people and send some to college while others were prevented from doing so and then watch their children to see how many from each group graduate from college. On the other hand, you could do a survey with a questionnaire that asked a large number of older people about their level of education and the level of education of their adult children.

The problem with such surveys is trying to assess what the results mean. Given a certain number of people surveyed, you might find that 75 percent of the children of college-educated parents graduated from college, whereas only 50 percent of the children of parents without a college education did so. Was the number of people surveyed large enough to allow you to say with a fair degree of certainty that children of college-educated people are more likely to become college graduates than those of parents who did not attend college? Only a statistical analysis of the data will provide an answer. Consequently, if you do a survey, you may need help from someone such as a math teacher to determine whether the results of your survey are significant.

On the other hand, a simple survey may provide results that need no evaluation. Suppose you conducted a survey to find out what foods students in your school prefer for lunch. You could give each student a questionnaire asking him or her to rate the foods on a scale of 1 to 4 in which 1 means, "like it very much"; 2 means, "like it"; 3 means, "do not like it but will eat it"; 4 means, "would never eat it." For each food, you could list your results and illustrate them in charts or graphs.

4

Planning the Project

Planning is not the part of your project that is the most fun, but it can save you a lot of time. It is worth doing thoroughly and carefully. Begin with a preliminary plan.

Why Plan?

The purpose of a plan is to avoid reaching a point in your project where you suddenly realize you cannot go on or that you will never finish by the time of the fair. Perhaps a piece of equipment that you need is too expensive or too complicated to use. Perhaps the experiment you want to do has to be done in the summer, and the fair will be held in the spring. The friend you were counting on to help you might move to another state.

As you develop a preliminary plan, be flexible. If the experiment you plan to do requires equipment you can't afford, do not give up.

If you plan to do an experiment in which you will need to record temperatures in a refrigerator or freezer, you will need more than a thermometer because you can't see through the doors. You may need a temperature probe with a wire running to a computer, or you might be able to use an indoor-outdoor thermometer. Your school might let you use the equipment you need, or you might come up with a similar experiment that requires less costly materials.

You may realize that you do not have enough time to complete the project. Will you do it anyway and present it at next year's fair, or will you abandon the idea and look for a topic that can be completed in the allotted time? All such problems can be avoided if you plan.

What Should a Plan Include?

You should start developing a plan as soon as you decide to do a project. The plan should include

- the purpose of your project.

- a description of what you are going to do.

- a list of all the materials you will need.

- a schedule showing the times when various parts of the project must be completed.

The Purpose

The first item in your plan is the *purpose* of your project. This can be a brief statement related to the question you want to answer or the problem you hope to solve. You can describe the report you plan to write, the demonstration you will do, the model you will build, the famous experiment you will carry out, or the survey you will conduct.

In the case of the pendulum experiment discussed in Chapter 3, the purpose might read as follows: "The purpose of my project is to find an answer to the question, How does the mass of the bob affect the period of a pendulum?" Then you might add your hypothesis: "The period of a pendulum increases as the mass of the bob increases." You might also include, "This hypothesis seems reasonable to me because I expect a large mass to move more sluggishly than a small one."

A Description of the Project

Write a complete description of what you plan to do. As you write it, you may realize that there are problems associated with your

48

project. Do not ignore these problems. Try to solve them now. If they can't be solved, you will save time and avoid wasted energy by modifying your project or changing your topic now. Experiments, models, and demonstrations all require materials. Are these materials readily available? Can you buy the things you need? Can you afford them? If not, can you borrow some of them from your school? Reports require sources of information. Are the books, magazines, or CD-ROMs that you need available at your library? If not, can your library obtain them from another library? Can you find any useful material on the Internet?

If you are doing an experiment, write out the details of the procedures you expect to follow, recognizing that you may need to make changes later. If you were doing the pendulum experiment discussed in Chapter 3, your description might look like the following:

- Build a pendulum like the one shown in Figure 3b (Chapter 3). The string can be clamped to the edge of a door frame.

- Connect a bob with a known mass to the lower end of the string. Adjust the length of the string until the distance between the clamp and the center of the bob is exactly 1.0 m. Keep this length constant throughout all the experiments.

- Pull the bob 10 cm to one side of its rest position and release it. Start a stopwatch at the same time. After the pendulum bob makes one complete swing back and forth, stop the watch and record the time. Repeat this several times to be sure the measurement is precise. If it is not, measure the time for the bob to make a number of swings and then divide the total time by the number of swings to find the period for one oscillation (swing).

- Repeat the experiment, using a bob with a different mass, and record its period. Do this for a number of different masses. Determine whether the pendulum's period increases as the mass of the bob increases.

- Repeat the entire experiment several times to be sure that the results are consistent. If possible, another person should do the experiment to be sure the results are not biased.

- In this experiment the independent variable is the mass of the bob. The dependent variable is the period of the pendulum. There should be no change in any of the other variables such as the length of the pendulum, the amplitude of the swing, the size of the bob, the location of the experiment, the temperature, the humidity, and so on.

A List of Materials

By making a list of the materials you need and a possible source for each one, you can determine whether or not all the materials can be obtained. Think carefully as you make your list. A balance that can weigh objects to the nearest gram is of little value if you need to determine masses or mass changes that are only tenths or hundredths of a gram. Similarly, a household thermometer that measures temperatures of -40 to 50°C (-40 to 120°F) is of no value if you plan to measure the temperature of boiling water (100°C, or 212°F).

Much of the equipment you need may be available in your home. You may be able to borrow some items from your school or local high school laboratories. Other items may have to be purchased at a hardware store, drugstore, or supermarket. Any technical supplies can be obtained from a science supply house. Your science teacher can probably provide a catalog for one or more of the science supply houses and help you place the order. Other places to look for materials you need are junkyards, lumberyards, and the industrial arts shop if your school has one. Because you will have to pay for supplies you buy, it is a good idea to make a list of the costs of these things to see whether you can afford everything you need. A list of the materials needed for the pendulum experiment described in the previous section is provided in Table 5.

Table 5: List of items needed for the pendulum project.

Item	Source	Cost
string (2 m)	in kitchen drawer	0
door frame or beam	my basement	0
4-inch C-clamp	Dad's workbench	0
bobs of different masses	School has some, or I can order them from a science supply house catalog.	$45.00
balance	school, or use Mom's postage scale	0
meterstick	school, or I can use a yardstick because 1.0 m = 3.28 ft (3 ft 3 3/8 in)	0
ruler (30 cm)	my desk	0
stopwatch	my soccer coach	0
a friend to repeat the experiments	Jill said she would help.	0

A Schedule

Like many other people, you might be in the habit of putting things off until the last minute. Such an approach will not work with a science fair project. To be sure your project is ready by the date of the science fair, you need to set up a schedule and meet the deadlines. The first item to place on your timeline is the final one, the one at the bottom of your schedule—the date of the science fair. That is a deadline you cannot avoid if you hope to participate. The next task is to divide the period between the time you begin working on the project and the date of the fair into a series of steps. For each step,

Table 6: Sample schedule for the pendulum project.

Work to accomplish	My deadline	Date due
Choose a topic for a project.	Oct. 23	Oct. 30
Write a hypothesis.	Nov. 7	
Prepare a preliminary plan.	Nov. 10	
Refine the topic if necessary.	Nov. 15	Nov. 21
Write out a detailed plan for the project.	Dec. 15	
Conduct experiments.	Jan. 15	
Have Jill repeat the experiments.	Jan. 29	
Analyze the experimental results.	Feb. 10	
Write a conclusion and suggest future experiments.	Feb. 17	
Write a rough draft of the report.	Mar. 10	
Prepare data tables, drawings, and graphs for display.	Mar. 24	
Write a second draft of the report.	Mar. 31	
Rewrite report based on Mom's and Jill's suggestions.	Apr. 6	
Write an abstract and introduction.	Apr. 10	
Build a backboard and display.	Apr. 24	
Prepare the oral presentation.	Apr. 27	
Revise oral presentation based on Dad's suggestions.	Apr. 28	
Set up exhibit.	Apr. 29	Apr. 29
Attend science fair and make presentation.	Apr. 30	Apr. 30

determine a reasonable length of time to get the job done and set a date by which to have it completed. Then meet or beat each deadline.

The schedule in Table 6 illustrates what a time frame might look like for the pendulum project. The schedule assumes that the fair is to be held on April 30 and a topic must be submitted by October 30 of the previous year.

5

Doing the Project

You have chosen a topic, refined it, and written a detailed explanation of how you plan to proceed. You have obtained the materials you need, developed a time frame, and have reached the point on your schedule where you have to do the work that constitutes the core of your project. If you are doing a report, you will probably spend a good deal of time at the library or working at a computer, downloading information from the Internet. Once you have obtained the information you need, you can do the actual writing at home. If you have access to a computer or word processor, you can do the writing electronically. A word-processing program will make it easier to change sentences; move paragraphs; check your spelling; make, cut, and paste drawings; and so on. Furthermore, when you complete your report, it can be printed in a neat and easy-to-read format.

Surveys will require you to spend time preparing questionnaires. You will need to test them on people, then conduct actual interviews of the people you plan to survey. If the survey is complicated, you will have to ask someone to help you evaluate the survey from a statistical standpoint.

Models, demonstrations, and experiments all require materials and a place where you can build things and test them or use them to conduct experiments. You will probably want a place where you can leave whatever you are working on without having it interfere with the activities of others. It might be your room if the project is not too large or messy. It could be your family's kitchen if you can easily put your equipment away. Be sure your experiment or construction will not affect others who have to use the kitchen for cooking, washing dishes, eating, and so on. A basement, garage, or porch is a good location for a project that requires a work space where something can be left and worked on from time to time, such as the construction of a sizable model or demonstration, or an ongoing experiment such as the germination of seeds or the growth of plants. In some cases, you will have to work on your project at school. A science teacher may provide you with the materials that you need but not allow you to remove them from the school. In that case you will have to figure out an arrangement to work on your project before or after school or during free time within the school day.

Recording What You Do and What You Find

When you start experimenting, you will need to keep a logbook. Write your name and phone number in it in case it gets lost. A bound notebook with lined pages adjacent to graph-lined pages works well. The graph paper will make it easy to make graphs, charts, tables, and diagrams that are related to data, and the lined adjacent page will make it easy to take notes (see Figure 4). Do not feel you have to be an artist to make drawings. Rough sketches are fine as long as they mean something to you. The lines on graph paper will help you make simple diagrams. If you have trouble drawing a part of the apparatus, make a cartoon bubble like the one shown in Figure 5 and write a description of the part. If you have a camera, photographs of your experiment and its equipment can be very useful. This is especially true if progression or growth is important, such

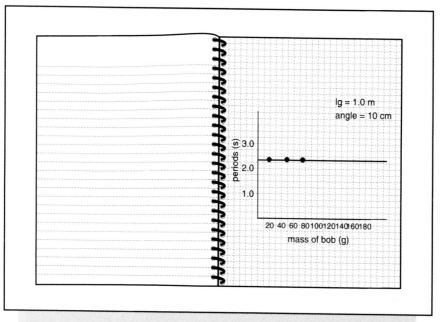

Figure 4. A notebook with graph paper on one side and lined pages on the other makes a useful logbook.

as the growth of plants or the metamorphosis of insects. Color prints may not be necessary; in fact, sometimes, black-and-white photographs are more useful. Attach small photographs or parts of proof sheets (if you have film developed professionally) to your logbook. Save the negatives; you may want to make larger prints to display when you set up your exhibit for the fair.

Write down everything you do in your logbook. Something that seems unimportant may be significant when you look back on it later. You may think you will remember everything you do or read, but you won't. We do so many things and so many things happen to us that we can't possibly remember all of them.

Each day you work on your project, write the date at the top of a page. Jot down notes as you work. Complete sentences are not necessary, and neatness is not essential. However, you should be able to read whatever you write. If you make a change, cross out

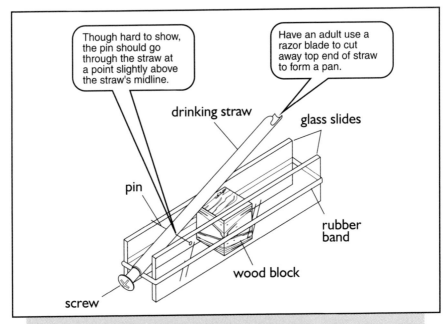

Figure 5. This drawing of a sensitive soda-straw balance shows how cartoon bubbles can be used to explain small parts of the drawing or parts that are difficult to draw.

the material, do not erase it. You might want to refer to the original. If you make drawings, diagrams, or graphs on an adjacent page, be sure to label them. What you write on one page may refer to the drawings and graphs on an adjacent page. For easy reference, number the pages. When you reach the point where you are ready to write the first draft of your report, it will be based on the information in your logbook so be sure you do not lose it. It is a good idea to leave your logbook with your experiment until the project is completed. You can then take it with you when you are ready to write the first draft of your report.

Do not be discouraged if your experiment does not turn out the way you expected. In the case of the pendulum project, the string supporting the bob might break, or you might be delayed by having to build your own balance and improvise weights because you can't afford them or can't borrow them from your school. The bobs may differ in size, forcing you to do an additional experiment to find out whether or not the size of the bob affects the period of the pendulum. Remember, judges look for creativity, innovative solutions, and an awareness of the scientific process. They will look favorably on your project if you recognized the need to carry out additional experiments or if you were innovative in building some of your own equipment. Realize, too, that even if your results do not agree with your hypothesis, the fact that you recognize and accept the negative findings of your experiments will be respected and well received by the judges.

Many things can happen that interfere with the best-laid plans for an experiment. The seeds you used might be old and fail to germinate; your dog might pull your bean plants out of the soil; you might drop a beaker containing the solution you have just filtered. More possible problems: The batteries you used to power your electrical apparatus might have been almost dead and stopped working during the night; the results of your experiment might not be what you expected; and so on. There is no end to the things that might go wrong. You might have to adjust your schedule to meet your deadlines; you might have to repeat part or all of your experiment; you might have to buy or find new materials. Be patient! After making the necessary adjustments, things might go better.

For the pendulum project, you might not be able to obtain bobs of different masses that are the same size. As a result, you would have to modify your project slightly. Perhaps size has no effect on the period of a pendulum. In that case, the bobs would not have to be identical in size. You could design another experiment in which you vary the size of the bob but keep the mass constant. You might use a tennis ball and a ball of clay of equal mass as bobs. If both bobs have the same period when the pendulums are of equal length and amplitude, then you will know that size is not related to the period of the pendulum. With that fact established, you could then use a set of weights to test the hypothesis that a pendulum's period increases with the mass of the bob. Even though the weights differ in size, if you kept the amplitude and the length between the point of support and the center of the weight constant, you could find out whether or not your hypothesis is correct.

You might be surprised to find that the period is the same regardless of the bob's mass. This would force you to rethink your hypothesis. Perhaps you would decide that since a baseball and a tennis ball fall at the same rate, it is reasonable to expect pendulum bobs to swing at the same rate. After all, a pendulum bob starts to fall, but because it is connected to a string, its path is restricted to an arc rather than to a straight-line fall. It is gravity that makes objects fall, and it is gravity that causes a pendulum bob to swing downward when you release it. Since gravity causes all objects to fall at the same rate, it is reasonable to expect pendulum bobs to move at the same rate regardless of their mass.

Measurements

Most scientific measurements are made using SI units (*Système International d'Unités*; International System of Units). Consequently, you should use these units when you make or report measurements associated with your project. There are seven basic SI units. Table 7 lists them and explains what they measure.

These basic units can be divided into smaller units, or multiples of these units can be expressed as a larger unit. Except for units of time, the larger or smaller units are always related to the basic units by multiples of 10 or 0.1 (1/10). For example, a meter is equal to 10 decimeters (dm), 100 centimeters (cm), and 1,000 millimeters (mm); a kilometer is equal to 1,000 meters, 10,000 decimeters, 100,000 centimeters, and 1,000,000 millimeters. Table 8 shows some of the relationships between the basic SI units and smaller and larger units in the same system.

The final digit of any measurement is always an estimate; no measurement is ever exact. For example, as you can see in Figure 6, the person measuring the length of the cubic block has to estimate

Table 7: Basic units used in the International System of Units (SI).

Unit	Abbreviation Measure	Used to Measure
meter	m	length
kilogram	kg	mass
second	s	time
ampere	A	electric current
kelvin	K	temperature
mole	mol	amount of substance (number of molecules)
candela	cd	luminance intensity

the final fraction of a millimeter. That person's estimate might be 1.87 cm, while yours might be 1.86 or 1.88 cm. Neither estimate can claim to be the exact length of the cube. In fact, it is probably not possible to estimate the length more accurately than to the nearest 0.2 mm. Consequently, you should probably record the length as whatever you estimate it to be plus or minus 0.2 mm or 0.02 cm. A shorthand way of doing this is to write 1.86 ± 0.02 cm. Someone reading such a record will understand what the limitation of the measurement was. If the measurement had been made using a ruler marked in centimeters but not millimeters, then the measurement would have been limited to plus or minus 0.1 cm. It would have been estimated to the nearest 0.1 cm and probably recorded as 1.8 ± 0.1 cm.

The basic SI units can be used to form what are called derived units. For example, the area of a floor could be expressed in meter x meter, or square meters (m^2). Similarly, volume can be expressed as meter x meter x meter, or cubic meters (m^3). Speed, which is measured in units of distance over time, would have units such as meters per second (m/s) or kilometers per hour (kph).

Table 8: Some relationships among commonly used units that are multiples or submultiples of the basic SI units of measure.

Unit	Abbreviation	Equivalent in basic units
1 nanometer	1 nm	0.000000001 m (10^{-9} m)
1 micrometer	1 μm	0.000001 m (10^{-6} m)
1 millimeter	1 mm	0.001 m (10^{-3} m)
1 centimeter	1 cm	0.01 m (10^{-2} m)
1 decimeter	1 dm	0.1 m (10^{-1} m)
1 kilometer	1 km	$1,000$ m (10^{3} m)

1 microgram	1 μg	0.000001 g (10^{-6} g) or 0.000000001 kg (10^{-9} kg)
1 milligram	1 mg	0.001 g (10^{-3} g) or 0.000001 kg (10^{-6} kg)
1 gram	1 g	0.001 kg (10^{-3} kg)

1 nanosecond	1 ns	0.000000001 s (10^{-9} s)
1 microsecond	1 μs	0.000001 s (10^{-6} s)
1 millisecond	1 ms	0.001 s (10^{-3} s)
1 minute	1 min	60 s
1 hour	1 hr	$3,600$ s
1 day	1 day	$86,400$ s

1 microampere	1 μA	0.000001 A (10^{-6} A)
1 milliampere	1 mA	0.001 A (10^{-3} A)

1 micromole	1 μmol	0.000001 mol (10^{-6} mol) or 6.02×10^{-17} molecules
1 millimole	1 mmol	0.001 mol (10^{-3} mol) or 6.02×10^{-20} molecules

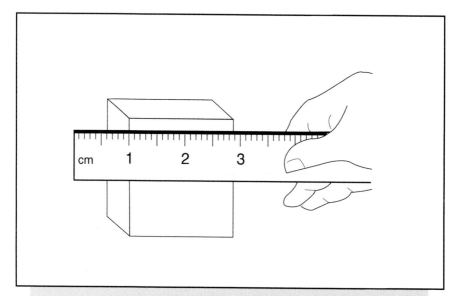

Figure 6. A ruler is placed across the top of a cube. What is your estimate of the cube's length? (Notice that the end of the ruler is not used in making measurements; the ends of rulers are often worn and rough.)

Controls

If your project involves experimentation, you must be ready to change the independent variable to see what effect it has on the dependent variable, as we saw in Chapter 3. At the same time, you must try to keep all the other variables constant. If you do experiments in physical science, such as the pendulum experiment discussed earlier, these tasks are generally not difficult. As long as you do the experiment in one location over a reasonably short time, you can be quite certain that variables such as temperature, gravity, light, and humidity are not going to change. Controlling variables is more difficult for experiments in other sciences such as biology, sociology, and psychology.

Suppose you want to investigate the effect of fertilizer X on the growth of plants. The independent variable would be the fertilizer added to the soil in which the plants grow, and the dependent variable is the growth of the plants, which can be determined by measuring their height or mass. However, to see what effect the fertilizer has, you will also need a set of control plants. These are plants to which no fertilizer is added. All other conditions, to the best of your ability, must be exactly the same. These other variables include temperature, the containers in which the plants grow, the amount of light and water the plants receive, and the soil in which they grow. Of course, all the plants should be of the same species.

The more plants you include in the experiment, the more certain you can be of the results. You might test 20 plants by adding 5 grams of fertilizer to the soil, another 20 by adding 10 grams of fertilizer, and a third group of 20 by adding 15 grams of fertilizer. These 60 plants would be the experimental plants. Another group of 20 plants would receive no fertilizer. These would be the control plants. All other factors should be identical for all the plants.

In conducting such an experiment, try to avoid any bias that would tend to favor your hypothesis. Do not give the experimental plants any more water than the controls. Do not place them where they receive more light or warmth than the controls. In selecting the seeds from which the two groups are grown, be sure to select the seeds randomly from the same package. Do not pick the small seeds to plant as the controls and use the larger ones to grow the experimental plants.

Suppose after six weeks you measure the plants and obtain the results shown in Table 9.

What conclusions would you reach based on these data?

In some experiments you might have to use two or more controls. For example, if you wanted to find out how two plants, such as radishes and tomatoes, compete when planted close to each other, you would need three sets of plants. In one container or section of a garden, you would plant radish and tomato seeds in an alternate manner. These seeds would grow into the experimental plants. To compare their growth with radish and tomato plants grown under

Table 9. The heights of plants receiving differing amounts of fertilizer.

Plant height with 5 g of fertilizer		Plant height with 10 g of fertilizer		Plant height with 15 g of fertilizer		Plant height with no fertilizer (controls)	
range (cm)	avg. (cm)	range (cm)	avg. (cm)	range (cm)	avg. (cm)	range (cm)	avg. (cm)
22.1– 25.4	23.5	24.1– 28.8	26.4	18.3– 20.8	19.9	20.5– 22.8	21.7

normal conditions, you would have to have two controls—one set of tomato plants and one set of radish plants—in which the plants do not compete. You would plant the seeds for the control plants at the same separation as the seeds for the experimental plants.

Strive to be objective at all times. Do not choose the best-looking or largest plants or seeds to serve as the experimental plants and the less healthy or smaller seeds to be the controls. Do not fail to record observations that throw suspicion on your hypothesis. Your hypothesis might have been wrong. Remember, there are no wrong results, but there may be plenty of unexpected ones. Mother Nature knows nothing of the ways we think she should behave!

Many discoveries have been made by accident. One of the most famous was Alexander Fleming's discovery of penicillin in 1928. Due to poor experimental technique, Fleming found that a mold was growing on one of his bacterial cultures. He was about to discard the culture when he noticed that there were no bacteria growing in the area surrounding the mold. Did the mold kill the bacteria? Fleming isolated the mold, which he identified as *Penicillium notatum*, and proceeded to grow cultures of it. He found that it would kill many kinds of bacteria but seemed to have no effect on animals or human red blood cells.

During World War II, there was a great need for a way to treat the bacterial infections that often developed in the wounds of soldiers injured in battle. After reading Fleming's account of his research, Dr. Howard Florey found that he could extract a substance that he called penicillin from a vat of *Penicillium notatum*. After successfully testing penicillin on animals and humans, the antibiotic penicillin was produced on a large scale. It was distributed to military hospitals throughout the world. Fleming's accidental discovery together with Florey's application led to the world's first antibiotic, a medicine that saved countless lives both during and after the war.

Wrap-Up Time

Once you complete your experiments, it is time to review all your notes, data tables, graphs, sketches, and anything else in your logbook. Based on all the work you have done, try to come to a conclusion or conclusions. If you had done the pendulum experiment described earlier, you would conclude that the period of a pendulum is independent of the mass of the bob. You would write that conclusion at the end of your logbook and describe the analysis that led you to it. You would also state that your results did not confirm your original hypothesis. Instead, they led you to rethink the false line of logic that led you to formulate that hypothesis.

You might go on to suggest additional experiments that would test the effect of other variables on the period of a pendulum. For example, is a pendulum's period affected by its length? Is it affected by the amplitude of the swinging bob?

Do not be surprised if you cannot reach any definite conclusion about the question or problem you are investigating. You won't be the first scientist to fail to reach a conclusion based on the data collected during experimentation. By doing the research, you learned a great deal about the process of science. Your investigation may also have prompted other questions. Be sure to include them in your logbook and final report.

Record and describe any errors that may have affected your results. Measurements are never perfect, no matter how careful you are. That is why it is wise to repeat an experiment as many times as possible and take an average of any quantitative results. As was mentioned earlier, it is also a good idea to follow any measurements with a plus or minus value (±) to indicate how accurately the measurement was estimated.

You may realize too late that a variable you thought had been controlled was a factor in the results you obtained. For example, if you were trying to find the effect of soil type on the growth of seedlings, you might have added equal amounts of water to the different soils. Later, you realized that because the water did not evaporate from the soils at the same rate, some seedlings received more water than other seedlings. Such errors should be included in your final report.

6

Writing the Report

Once you have completed your experimental work and have drawn whatever conclusions you can, you are ready to begin writing the first draft of your report. I say first draft because any well-written document should be revised several times before it is considered finished.

The lengthiest reports are usually those that involve original research. Regardless of the type of project or the length of the report, try to make it interesting. If you repeat a famous experiment, you might explain how the experiment could be done in other ways. Describe how the same experiment can be done today, using modern equipment not available to the original scientist. If you constructed a model, include the original plans or blueprints. Photographs can be used to show the model at various stages of its construction. Research based on reading might be enhanced by photographs, artwork, drawings, cartoons, and other illustrations.

The required contents of a final report are often provided at the time you submit a topic for a project, if not earlier. Generally, reports on any original research should include the following:

- title page;

- acknowledgments page, listing people who helped you;

- table of contents;

- abstract;

- statement of the problem or question under investigation;

- brief review of the references you used;

- statement of your hypothesis;

- list of the variables being considered;

- experimental procedure you followed;

- results, including observations, data charts and graphs, photographs, and drawings;

- analysis and conclusions with suggestions for possible further work on the topic;

- bibliography.

Title Page

The title page is the first thing a judge or someone else visiting your exhibit will read. The title of your project should be written in large letters near the top of the page. The name of your school's science fair and the date of the fair should also be included. Some science fairs require that you not place your name on the title page. This is to avoid any bias should one or more of the judges know you. A sample title page for the pendulum project mentioned earlier is given in Figure 7.

Acknowledgments

If there were people who helped you with your project, you should thank them on a page set aside for this purpose. In the case of pendulum project, the acknowledgments page might read as follows:

How Does the Mass of the Bob Affect the Period of a Pendulum?

An Experimental Investigation for

The Seaward Middle School's Science Fair

April 30, 2002

I am indebted to my father, who let me use some of the equipment needed for this experiment and who also helped me with my oral presentation; to my mother, who loaned me her postage scale and made valuable suggestions after reading my paper and correcting some misspellings; to my soccer coach, Mortimer Smith, who let me use his stopwatch; to my friend Jill Jones, who repeated my experiments and offered valuable suggestions; and to my science teacher, Ms. Jamella McArthur, who helped me understand the meaning of experimental and controlled variables.

Table of Contents

The last thing you will write is the table of contents, because it cannot be done before you have numbered the pages. The numbers can be placed at the bottoms or tops of the pages. Often, they are placed at the center of the bottom of each page or in the upper right-hand corner of each page. Numbering begins with the abstract. The title page, acknowledgments page, and table of contents are generally not numbered. The table of contents for the pendulum project is shown in Figure 8.

Abstract

The abstract is a one-page description of the project. It is one of the last things you will write and can be done after you have completed the rest of the report. An example of an abstract based on the pendulum project is provided here.

Abstract:

The question I investigated was, *How does the mass of the bob affect the period of a pendulum?* My hypothesis was, *The period of a pendulum increases as the mass of the bob increases.*

To test this hypothesis, I first had to show that the period did not depend on the size of the bob. I did this by using a tennis ball and a clay ball as bobs. The tennis ball was larger than the ball of clay, but both had the same mass. I measured their periods after being certain that the lengths of the pendulums and amplitudes of swing were the same. I found the periods to be very nearly the same. I then used bobs of different masses and measured the period of the pendulum for each

Table of Contents

Figure 8. An example of a table of contents for a science fair report is shown.

different mass, being careful to keep all other variables constant. The results of these experiments showed that my hypothesis was not correct. The period of a pendulum does not depend on the mass of the bob. Even when the mass of the bob was increased by more than four times, the period did not change.

Question

The question or problem should be asked or stated clearly in one sentence if possible. It would be the same question that is found in the abstract. Both the independent and dependent variables should be included in the wording of the question or problem. In the case of the pendulum project, the question would be, "How does the mass of the bob affect the period of a pendulum?" It includes the independent variable (the mass of the bob) and the dependent variable (the period of the pendulum).

Review of the Literature

If your project is based on research about some aspect of science, then your report will essentially be a review of the materials you have read. If it is part of a research project involving experimentation, it will be a summary of the material you have read that is related to your experiment. The review should be in your own words. If you want to include the exact words of something you have read, you will need to enclose those words in quotation marks and give credit to the author. You can do this by typing a small superscript number after the quotation. The same number is placed at the bottom of the page, followed by the citation, starting with the author's name. If the quote is from a book, the book's title, in italic type, should follow the author's name. Next, the place of publication should be listed, followed by the name of the publisher, the date of publication, the volume (if given), and the page number. For example, if you quoted something from this book, the footnote might look like this:

1. Robert Gardner, *Science Fair Projects—Planning, Presenting, Succeeding* (Springfield, N.J.: Enslow Publishers, Inc., 1999), p. 24.

If the quote is from an article, the title of the article should follow in quotation marks, then the name of the periodical, in italic type, in which the article appeared. It should also include the volume number, date of publication, and page numbers. A typical footnote for a quotation from a magazine would look like this:

1. Sheryl Gay Stolberg, "Superbugs," *The New York Times Magazine*, August 2, 1998, p. 42.

For additional information about footnoting, you might consult a handbook of composition or your English teacher.

In the case of the pendulum project, the experimenter did relatively little research by reading. Instead, the young scientist tested the hypothesis by experimentation. The following example using the hypothetical pendulum project reflects the experimenter's decision.

Review of the Literature

I decided not to do an extensive review of the literature because I wanted to test my hypothesis by doing my own experiments without knowing what someone else had discovered. I had heard that Galileo was the first person to investigate pendulums, and I read an account of his life by Isaac Asimov (see bibliography).

While attending church as a teenager, Galileo noticed that the chandeliers appeared to swing back and forth at a steady rate. To test this idea, he used his pulse to see if the period was really constant. "Upon returning home, he set up two pendulums of equal length and swung one in larger, one in smaller sweeps. They kept together and he found he was correct."[1]

1. Isaac Asimov, *Asimov's Biographical Encyclopedia of Science and Technology* (Garden City, N.Y.: Doubleday, 1964), pp. 71–75.

Hypothesis

In this section of your report, you state your hypothesis, which you formulate as a reasonable answer or solution to the question or problem. Bear in mind that your hypothesis is a guess—a reasonable and educated one, but nevertheless a guess—that must be checked by experiment.

In the case of the pendulum project, the question was, "How does the mass of the bob affect the period of a pendulum?" The hypothesis, which would be stated in this section, was, "The period of a pendulum increases as the mass of the bob increases."

Variables

Everyone using the scientific method agrees that an experiment should test only one variable at a time. That variable, the independent variable, is changed to see what effect it has on the dependent variable. In the pendulum project, the mass of the bob was changed, then a stopwatch was used to see if the period of the pendulum had changed. All the other variables were kept constant. For this example, the variables section would probably look like the following:

> Variables
> The independent variable in my experiment was the mass of the bob. It was changed to see what effect it had on the dependent variable, which was the period of the pendulum. To the best of my ability, all the other variables, such as the pendulum's length and amplitude, were kept constant. Since the experiments were always done in the same place over a reasonably short period of time, I believe such variables as temperature, humidity, location, light, air pressure, and any other variables were also controlled.

Procedure

When you were planning your project, you wrote out a procedure for doing the experiments. In doing the experiments, you probably made some changes. Things seldom proceed exactly as planned. Consequently, after doing the experiments, you can write a better procedure. Anyone who wants to repeat your experiment could do so simply by following the directions in this section of your report.

You might begin the procedure section by listing all the materials that are needed to do the experiments. For the pendulum project, the materials list might look like this:

Materials needed: a string more than 1 m long, a door frame or beam, a 4-inch C-clamp, pendulum bobs of different masses, a balance to weigh bobs, a meterstick or yardstick (1.0 m = 3.28 ft or 39 3/8 in), a ruler (30 cm), a stopwatch, a logbook to record data.

The procedure might be similar to the following sample.

1. Build a pendulum like the one shown in the drawing. (Include a drawing similar to Figure 3b in Chapter 3.) The string can be clamped to the edge of a door frame or beam. If you have access to laboratory apparatus for suspending objects on strings, you can use that. (See Figure 9.)

2. If you have bobs of identical size that are made of different metals, attach the lightest one to the end of the string. If you are using bobs of different sizes, do the same. (From another experiment I did, I know that the size of the bob has no effect on the period of a pendulum.)

3. Adjust the length of the string until the distance between the point where the string is clamped and the center of the bob is exactly 1.0 m. Keep this length constant throughout all the experiments.

4. Pull the bob 10 cm to one side of its rest position and release it. At the same time start a stopwatch. After the pendulum bob makes 20 complete swings, over and back, stop the watch and record the time. Do this several times to be sure the measurements are precise.

5. Repeat the experiment, using several bobs, each with a different mass. Record the pendulum's period for each of these different masses. For each experiment, be sure that the length of the pendulum from the point where the string is clamped to the center of the bob is exactly 1.0 m. Start the experiment by pulling the bob exactly 10 cm to one side so that the amplitude of the pendulum's swing is the same for each experiment.

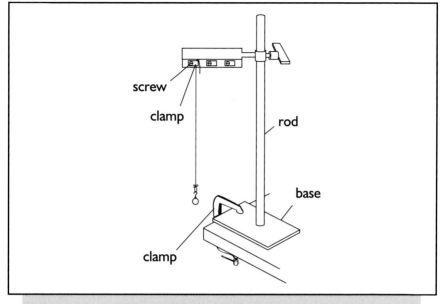

Figure 9. This type of laboratory stand can be used to suspend a pendulum.

Results

After explaining the procedure, report the results you obtained. You should include any pertinent observations, data tables, and graphs, drawings, and photographs, as well as a summary of the results. There is no need to interpret your results in this section; leave the analysis for your conclusion. If you are aware of errors, flaws, or data that you can't explain, be sure to mention them here. For example, in the pendulum project, the experimenter found that a single swing of the pendulum was too short to measure accurately. By timing 20 swings, the error involved in starting and stopping the watch became insignificant.

Tables 1, 2, 3, and 4 in Chapter 3 can serve as examples of the way your data should appear in your report. If you draw reasonably well, line sketches may help in reporting your results. If you have difficulty drawing, you might ask a friend to help you, and give that person credit in your acknowledgments.

The graph in Figure 4 (Chapter 5) is an example of the way data can be presented. The usual practice, as shown in that graph, is to plot values for the independent variable on the horizontal axis. The corresponding values for the dependent variable are plotted on the vertical axis. For some experiments or projects, other graphical representations may be more appropriate. Some examples of other types of graphs are shown in Figure 10.

Conclusions

Begin this section of your report by repeating your hypothesis and then stating whether or not your results support or reject the hypothesis. Analyze the data and explain what, if anything, your results indicate. Do not be afraid to admit that your experimental results do not support your hypothesis. A good scientist has to accept nature as it is, not as he or she thinks it should be.

If you see that your results have applications in other areas, be sure to mention them. If, as a result of your experimental work, you see a better way to carry out your experiment, be sure to include it. Similarly, you may now be thinking about additional experiments that could be done to extend or enhance the work you have accomplished. Include tentative designs for those experiments in your concluding remarks. They will be well received by judges and may be the basis for another science project. A sample conclusion for the pendulum project follows.

Conclusion and Further Study
My hypothesis was that the period of a pendulum will increase as the mass of the bob increases. The results of my experiments do not support my hypothesis. The data show that increasing the mass of the bob from 18 grams to 76 grams had no significant effect on the period of the pendulum. The period remained almost the same regardless of the bob's mass. Therefore, I conclude that my hypothesis was wrong. The period of a pendulum is not affected by the mass of the bob.

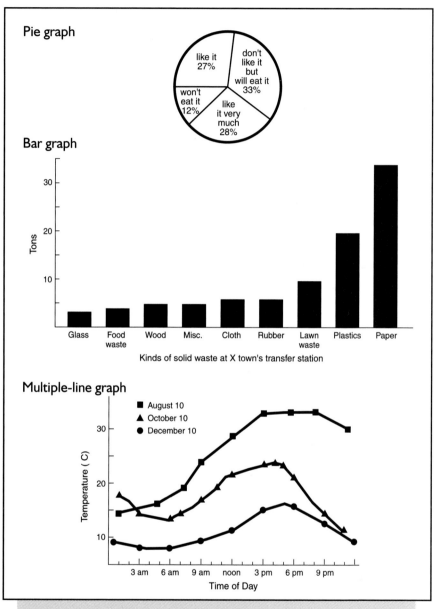

Figure 10. Several types of common graphs are shown here. You many want to use these and others in preparing a science fair report. In multiple-line graphs, the separate lines may be identified as shown or by color, label, or different patterns such as solid line, dashed line, dotted line, and so on.

I think the reason the period is not affected by the bob's mass is related to the fact that reasonably heavy objects all fall at the same rate. A pendulum bob is much like a falling object except that the string prevents it from falling straight down.

Because a pendulum's period is constant, pendulums were used as clocks for many years. Many homes still have such clocks. They are called grandfather clocks. However, I do not think pendulum clocks on the moon would agree with pendulum clocks on the earth. It is gravity that makes the pendulum bob move, and gravity on the moon is only one sixth as strong as gravity on the earth. Therefore, I think a pendulum's period would be longer on the moon than it is on the earth. If astronauts ever land on the moon again, they might compare a pendulum's period there with its period on the earth. I think they would find its period is longer on the moon than on the earth.

Having found that the mass of a pendulum bob has no effect on the pendulum's period, there are other independent variables I might test to see whether they change the period of a pendulum. I have already found that the size of the bob has no effect on the period, but there are other experiments that might be tried. Does the length of a pendulum affect its period? This could be tested by changing the pendulum's length and measuring the period for each length. Similarly, the amplitude could be changed to see whether it has any effect on the period.

I do not think amplitude will affect the period. The pendulum appeared to swing back and forth at the same rate regardless of how far it moved. On the other hand, I noticed that it appeared to swing a lot faster when I shortened the string, so I think a pendulum's period is affected by its length, but I do not know exactly how they are related. Perhaps, as a science project for next year, I will try to find out.

Bibliography

The bibliography should include all the books and articles you read, as well as any people you interviewed. The author's name (last name first) should be followed by the book's italicized title. Next comes the place of publication, the publisher, and the year the book was published. For example:

Adams, Richard, and Robert Gardner. *Ideas for Science Projects.* Revised Edition. Danbury, Conn.: Franklin Watts, Inc., 1997.

Here is the format for magazine articles:

Author's name (last name first). "Title of the Article" (in quotation marks). *Name of the Magazine* (underlined or italicized), Date of publication, volume number, and pages covered by the article.

For an encyclopedia or a book without a specific author, the italicized name of the encyclopedia or book is written first, followed by the place of publication, the publisher, the year published, the volume number, and the pages you used.

Internet sites should also be included in your bibliography. Here is the format:

Author's name (last name first). "Title of document (in quotation marks)." *Title of complete work* (italicized). Date of publication or last revision if known. <Web address (in brackets)> (Date you visited the site, in parentheses).

If you interview people, they should be listed (last name first) in alphabetical order within your bibliography, together with his or her occupation, the city and state where the person lives, and the date (month, day, year) of the interview.

A Final Word

If you have access to a computer or word processor, try to use either to write your report. It will be much easier to make changes as you revise the paper. The report should be double-spaced on 8 1/2 by 11-inch paper with one-inch margins. After you finish the first draft, take a break. Return to the report rested, refreshed, and ready to read it critically. As you rework what you have written, eliminate words, sentences, even paragraphs that are not needed. Make it as concise as possible. Rewrite sentences to improve clarity and grammar. Many people find it helps to read the report aloud. Your ear may be better than your eyes at catching grammatical errors, ambiguities, and poorly worded sentences.

After you have rewritten the report several times, ask someone else to read it with a critical eye. If possible, have both your English and science teachers read it and make suggestions. Listen carefully to criticisms and suggestions. The readers are trying to help you produce a better report.

7

Exhibiting the Project

Most science fairs have rules about the amount of space you will have to display your work. Before you begin building your display or exhibit, check to see what those dimensions are. Generally, you will have a space that extends upward about 122 cm (48 in) from a tabletop, is about 75 cm (30 in) deep, and is about 122 cm (48 in) wide. The most common format consists of three panels—a wide central panel flanked by two wing panels of equal height. The panels can be made from triwall or corrugated cardboard, plywood, Peg-Board, or particleboard. Tape or hinges can be used to hold the panels upright and allow them to be folded for transport to the exhibition. Before you begin building the panels, you should make a scaled (1:10) drawing of your plan for a display.

Preparing the Exhibit

Large colored letters, photographs, and drawings will help make your exhibit attractive. You can print large colored labels if you have access to a computer and a color printer. Alternatively, you can buy such letters at an art supply store or cut them from magazines or construction paper. The panels can be covered with paint, felt, cloth, sheets, or paper. The items that you display will depend on the nature of your project. If your project was limited to reading research, you will want to enliven your display with color photographs and drawings from articles you read. Large print to emphasize key or unusual facts will add interest to your exhibit. Projects involving experiments or models should include the equipment used or the model if possible. If not, a scaled representation or large photographs of the featured materials should be displayed.

An exhibit of a research project involving experimental work should include statements of the original question or problem, the hypothesis, the materials and other details about the procedure used in the experiments, the results of the experiments, including data tables and graphs, diagrams, observations, charts, and conclusions based on the data. If possible, the experimental setup can be displayed on the table. Figure 11 shows how the pendulum project might appear as an exhibit. Bear in mind that hazardous materials cannot be part of your exhibit. Check the rules carefully and be certain you do not have chemicals or electrical circuits that will lead officials to disqualify your display.

Be careful not to clutter your display. Too much material will detract from the main theme of your project. A few well-chosen items, an appealing title, statements with large print, and a colorful background will attract visitors. Those who are truly interested in your topic can find the details in your report and logbook, which should be on the table, or by talking to you.

The Oral Presentation

Prepare what you plan to say to the judges well before you set up your exhibit. Rehearse your presentation in front of a mirror and with a tape recorder. Practice eye contact by looking into the eyes of your mirror image. Use gestures, change the level of your voice, and be enthusiastic about what you have done. After listening to your recorded words, you will probably want to make a number of

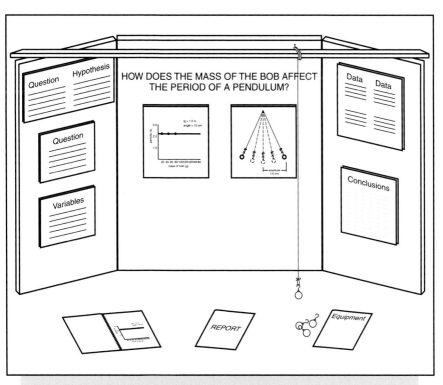

Figure 11. An exhibit of an experimental project at a science fair is shown. This one is for the pendulum project used as an example in this book.

changes and practice some more. Then, ask a friend or parent to listen to your talk and to offer suggestions about how you might improve it.

Whatever you do, do not memorize your presentation so that it sounds like a canned speech, and do not read it. A few notes written or printed on a file card to remind you of key points and the sequence of things you want to mention are fine. You can glance at these notes as you speak, and you can maintain interest by pointing to parts of your exhibit that illustrate your words. (Figure 12 shows some notes that might be used by an experimenter who did the pendulum project.) Remember, you know more about your project than anyone else, so relax and enjoy the opportunity to explain what you did and what you found.

> Notes for Presentation
> Introduce self
> Source of idea for pendulum project
> Question
> Hypothesis
> Experiment to show that size
> of bob not important
> Variables and Procedure used
> Results
> Conclusion
> Possible extensions
> Questions

Figure 12. Notes for an oral presentation prepared by someone exhibiting the pendulum project are shown.

Some Helpful Hints

The words you use in your report and presentation are important, but so are your appearance and manner. The following suggestions will help you make a favorable impression on the judges.

- Stand to one side of the exhibit. Do not block the view of your display and the things you want to point out.

- Stand erect and on both feet. Do not sway from side to side as you talk.

- Be well dressed and well groomed.

- Maintain eye contact with the judges, but do not stare.

- Be ready to smile or laugh, but do not paste on a fake smile.

- Be polite and well mannered. For example, do not chew gum or eat while you talk.

- Try to involve the judges in your project. Point out parts of your display as you talk to them.

- Give judges and other visitors the opportunity to ask questions.

- Respond to questions with honest answers. If you do not know the answer to a question, say so, do not try to fake it. You can, of course, express an opinion or venture a guess based on what you have learned, but make it clear that you cannot speak with certainty.

- Speak up! There will be unavoidable background noise at the fair. People won't be able to hear you if you speak softly.

- Talk slowly. Your listeners will not be as familiar with your project as you are.

- Thank the judges at the conclusion of your presentation.

Whether Prizes or Not

The experience of exhibiting your project at a science fair will give you an opportunity to see what other students have done. Tour the

Whether you win first prize at the fair, as Laurie Rabinowitz and Robert Brenner did, or whether you don't, participating in your school's science fair will be a rewarding experience.

fair. Talk to other presenters. Their projects may give you an idea for a future project. Listen to the judges. They may offer suggestions that will enable you to develop a better project for next year's fair.

By following the suggestions offered in this book, you may bring a blue-ribbon project to your school's science fair and perhaps go on to a state or national fair. Winning a prize at the fair would be a welcome and rewarding end to all your hard work. However, even if you do not win a prize, you will have learned a lot about science and the topic you investigated. You will also have developed a number of skills that will be useful throughout your life—thinking, planning, organizing, writing, building, communicating, and, most important, learning how to find answers for yourself.

8

Alternatives to Science Fairs

In some schools, invention fairs, or invention conventions, as they are sometimes called, have replaced or have been added to the annual science fair. Other events for science students include local science Olympiads, symposiums, and expositions. If you have success at local science events, you might think about entering a national or international event such as the Intel Science Talent Search or the International Science and Engineering Fair (see page 97).

Invention Fairs and Lateral Thinking

An invention fair is usually much less formal than most science fairs. There is no need for a formal report showing how you followed the scientific method in developing your invention. The exhibit consists of the invention along with a brief report. If the device you invent is too large for the display booth, a smaller working model can be made. While the exhibits are similar to those found at science fairs, each report simply describes the invention, the purpose it serves, and, perhaps, how the inventor arrived at the idea.

The creativity and innovative thinking associated with an invention can reveal a spark of genius in a young mind. One skill developed by those who participate in invention fairs is the ability to think laterally. Lateral thinking involves making associations and seeing connections between ideas and things normally regarded as unrelated. It is a trait that inventors seem to share with scientists and detectives. One example is the way Friedrich Kekule (1829–1896) came up with the structure of the benzene molecule. Chemists knew that the chemical formula for benzene was C_6H_6, but no one had been able to explain how the atoms could be arranged. Carbon has a valence of four—it combines with four hydrogen atoms to form methane (CH_4) or with two oxygen atoms to form carbon dioxide (CO_2). One night Kekule, who had puzzled over benzene's structure for some time, had a dream. In his dream, he saw a ring of snakes attached head to tail rolling down a hill. Kekule awoke with an understanding of the structure of benzene. He saw it as a ring of carbon atoms (the snakes in his dream) with a hydrogen attached to each carbon as shown in Figure 13. Alternate carbons formed double bonds with other carbon atoms. To critics who asked how the carbon atoms could "know" which ones were to have double bonds, Kekule argued that the double bonds shifted back and forth between alternate carbon atoms.

Olympiads: Team and Individual Science Competition

Some school districts organize science teams within each school that compete with teams from other schools. Such events are sometimes called Olympiads or science bowls. For example, a competing biology team might use a field guide to identify trees to which the teachers organizing the meet have attached numbered tags. A physics or physical science team might be given a number of items

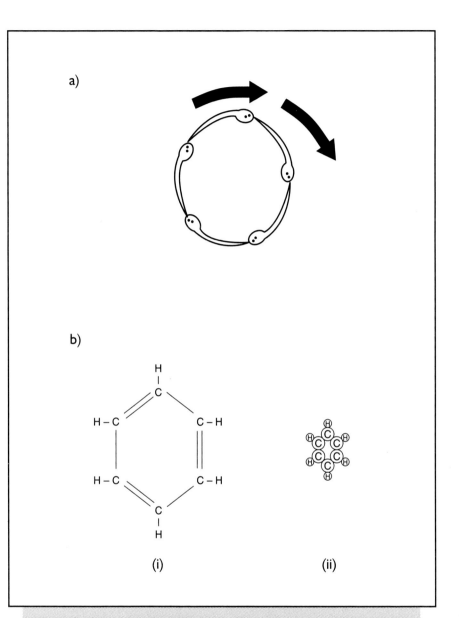

a)

b)

(i)   (ii)

Figure 13. a) Kekule dreamed of a ring of snakes rolling down a hill. b) (i) Kekule's structural arrangement of the atoms in a benzene molecule (C_6H_6) is shown. Each line represents a chemical bond between atoms. Carbon has a valence of four. Note that each carbon atom has four bonds. (ii) This drawing shows how the actual molecule might look.

such as a yardstick, paper plates, string, a drill, and twisties, with the task of building a balance that can weigh as accurately as possible. Each team might then be asked to weigh an object. The winning team would be the one that most accurately determines the object's mass.

Examples of more general events might include ones in which teams invent a device that can be used for a specific purpose, use toothpicks to build a bridge that can support the most weight, or devise a method for measuring something that is very large or very small. There might also be a Jeopardy-type quiz in which individuals or teams compete in answering science trivia questions.

Individual competition can include dropping eggs from a specified height in break-proof cartons designed by the students, keeping an ice cube from melting for the longest time, making a paper airplane that flies the farthest or for the longest time, and so on.

At some Olympiads or science expositions, students compete in written and verbal quizzes as well as in science activities. The activities might include estimating the number of beans in a jar, determining the density of an irregular object, determining the thickness of a sheet of aluminum foil, using a balance and a ruler, or classifying various plants and animals.

A science meet or Olympiad often concludes with a social hour where students or teams from different schools meet, chat, and enjoy refreshments. While the students eat and socialize, their work is being judged by some of the teachers. Following the social period, prizes and trophies are awarded to the winning teams.

National and International Science Fairs and Events

If you have enjoyed working on projects for science fairs or other science competitions or events, you might like to move on to the national level, where you could win a scholarship or become eligible to work with scientists on a part-time basis. Information about the opportunity to exercise your science, engineering, or inventive talents on the national level can be obtained by contacting one or more of the organizations listed on page 97.

Should you desire to enter truly competitive science fairs, consider entering your project in the Science Talent Search or ISEF. Do you like working with a team of fellow students in solving problems and answering difficult questions related to science and scientific inquiry? If you do, organize a team and enter the Science Olympiad competition. If you are fascinated by space science, develop an experiment that can be carried out by astronauts on the space shuttle and enter it through NSTA/NASA. If you like to write, you will enjoy competing in the DuPont Science Essay. Are you imaginative? Do you enjoy tinkering and building gadgets that require batteries (electric cells)? If your answer is *yes*, you might like to seek one of the scholarships provided by Duracell/NSTA. Would you like to work with scientists engaged in research and find out what real science is like? Earthwatch, The National Science Foundation, and the Jackson Laboratory provide the opportunity to do so.

Science Competitions
and Organizations

Bayer/NSF Award for Community Innovation
105 Terry Drive
Suite 120
Newton, PA 18940
(800) 291-6020
http://www.nsf.gov/od/lpa/events/awards.htm
Competition open to students in grades 6–8 for designing or
improving a project that benefits the community.

The DuPont Science Essay
General Learning Corporation
900 Skokie Boulevard #200
Northbrook, IL 60062
(847) 205-3000
http://www.iasf.org/dupont.htm
Participants write an essay on a scientific topic and explain how it
will have an effect on society.

Duracell/NSTA Scholarships
National Science Teachers Association
Duracell/NSTA Scholarship Competition
1840 Wilson Boulevard
Arlington, VA 22201-3000
(703) 243-7100
http://www.nsta.org
http://iasf.org/duracell.htm
Students are encouraged to invent devices that use electric cells.
Scholarship money is awarded to winners.

Earthwatch
Student Challenge Awards Program
680 Mt. Auburn Street
PO Box 9104
Watertown, MA 02272
(617) 927-8200
http://www.earthwatch.org
Provides internships with research scientists engaged in various projects throughout the world.

Intel International Science and Engineering Fair (ISEF)
Science Service, Inc.
1719 N Street NW
Washington, D.C. 20036
(202) 785-2255
http://www.sciserv.org
General Motors and many other organizations work together to sponsor this fair. Projects may be in one of twelve categories ranging from computers to zoology.

Jackson Laboratory, Summer Student Program
Jackson Laboratory
Summer Student Program
600 Main Street
Bar Harbor, ME 04609-1500
(207) 288-6000
Participants work with scientists engaged in biological research at the Jackson Lab in Bar Harbor, Maine.

The National Science Foundation
4201 Wilson Boulevard
Arlington, VA 22230
(703) 306-1234
http://www.nsf.gov
Offers science training at a number of schools, colleges, and laboratories during the summer.

NSTA/NASA Science
National Science Teachers Association
1840 Wilson Boulevard
Arlington, VA 22201-3000
(703) 243-7100
http://www.nsta.org/programs/ssip.shtml
Students in grades 6 to 12 have an opportunity to design experiments that can be carried out on board the space shuttle.

Science Olympiad
National Office
Science Olympiad
5955 Little Pine Lane
Rochester, MI 48306
(248) 651-4013
http://www.macomb.k12.mi.us/science/olympiad.htm
Teams of students compete in written tests and various science activities requiring experimental technique and analysis.

Science Talent Search
Science Service
1719 N Street NW
Washington, D.C. 20036
(202) 785-2255
http://www.sciserv.org
The contest involves independent research in the sciences, including the social sciences as well as mathematics and engineering for students who are seniors in secondary school. Winners of this competition receive college scholarships.

Further Reading

Books

Adams, Richard, and Robert Gardner. *Ideas for Science Projects, Revised Edition*. Danbury, CT: Franklin Watts, Inc., 1997.

Asimov, Isaac. *Asimov's Biographical Encyclopedia of Science and Technology*. 2nd revised edition. Garden City, NY: Doubleday, 1982.

Barr, George. *Science Research Experiments for Young People*. New York: Dover, 1989.

Bochinski, Julianne Blair. *The Complete Handbook of Science Fair Projects*. New York: Wiley, 1996.

Bombaugh, Ruth J. *Science Fair Success, Revised and Expanded*. Springfield, NJ: Enslow Publishers, Inc., 1999.

Gardner, Robert. *Experimenting with Inventions*. New York: Franklin Watts, Inc., 1990.

———. *Famous Experiments You Can Do*. New York: Franklin Watts, Inc., 1990.

———. *More Ideas for Science Projects*. New York: Franklin Watts, Inc., 1989.

Krieger, Melanie Jacobs. *How to Excel in Science Competitions, Revised and Updated*. Springfield, NJ: Enslow Publishers, Inc., 1999.

Markle, Sandra. *The Young Scientist's Guide to Successful Science Projects*. New York: Lothrop, Lee, and Shepard, 1990.

Newton, David E. *Making and Using Scientific Equipment*. New York: Franklin Watts, 1993.

Provenzo, Eugene F., and Asterei Baker Provenzo. *47 Easy-to-Do Classic Science Experiments*. New York: Dover, 1989.

Sobey, Ed. *How to Enter and Win an Invention Contest*. Springfield, NJ: Enslow Publishers, Inc., 1999.

Tocci, Salvatore. *How to Do a Science Fair Project*. Revised Edition. Danbury, CT: Franklin Watts, Inc., 1997.

Internet Addresses

To Ask a Question:

The MAD Scientist Network. "Ask a Scientist." *The MAD Scientist Network*. August 18, 1998. <http://www.madsci.org> (August 18, 1998).

Guide to doing science projects:

Morano, David. *Experimental Science Projects: An Introductory Level Guide*. May 27, 1995. <http://www.isd77.k12.mn.us/resources/cf/SciProjIntro.html> (August 20, 1998).

For other ideas and resources:

Hart, Murray. "Science Fair Projects and Science Fairs." *The Science Page*. August, 1998. <http://www.techplus.com/scipage/scifair.htm> (August 18, 1998).

Index